Experiments with Sound and Hearing

By Chris Woodford

Please visit our Web site www.garethstevens.com. For a free color catalog of all our high-quality books, call toll free 1-800-542-2595 or fax 1-877-542-2596.

Library of Congress Cataloging-in-Publication Data
Woodford, Chris.
Experiments with sound and hearing / Chris Woodford.
p. cm. -- (Cool science)
Includes index.
ISBN 978-1-4339-3456-8 (library binding) -- ISBN 978-1-4339-3457-5 (pbk.)
ISBN 978-1-4339-3458-2 (6-pack)
1. Sound--Experiments--Juvenile literature. 2. Hearing--Experiments--Juvenile literature. I. Title.
QC225.5.W683 2010
534.078--dc22 2009041578

Published in 2010 by
Gareth Stevens Publishing
111 East 14th Street, Suite 349
New York, NY 10003

For Gareth Stevens Publishing:
Art Direction: Haley Harasymiw
Editorial Direction: Kerri O'Donnell

For The Brown Reference Group Ltd:
Editorial Director: Lindsey Lowe
Managing Editor: Tim Harris
Editor: Sarah Eason
Children's Publisher: Anne O'Daly
Design Manager: David Poole
Designer: Paul Myerscough
Production Director: Alastair Gourlay

Picture Credits:
Front Cover: Shutterstock: Corepics (foreground); dwphotos (background)
Title Page: Shutterstock: dwphotos
Shutterstock: 4, Gerrit 6t, Svemir 5, Suzanne Tucker 6b, SVLumagraphica 7
All other images Martin Norris

Publisher's note to educators and parents: Our editors have carefully reviewed the Web sites that appear on p. 31 to ensure that they are suitable for students. Many Web sites change frequently, however, and we cannot guarantee that a site's future contents will continue to meet our high standards of quality and educational value. Be advised that students should be closely supervised whenever they access the Internet.

Manufactured in the United States of America
1 2 3 4 5 6 7 8 9 12 11 10

CPSIA compliance information: Batch #BRW0102GS: For further information contact Gareth Stevens, New York, New York at 1-800-542-2595.

Contents

Introduction

Every time something moves it makes a sound, from the gentle flapping of a butterfly's wings to the noisy roar of a jet airplane taking off. Sounds are vibrations in the air. Our ears pick up the vibrations, and our brain interprets them as different sounds.

The sound of the jet engines of supersonic airplanes, such as the Concorde, is very loud.

The world is full of different sounds. We use sound to communicate by talking to each other. We listen to jokes and laugh with friends and sing and make different sounds on instruments to produce music. We also use sound to sense danger and react quickly. Many other animals use sound, too, from the beautiful sound of birdsong at dawn to the warning sound of a rattlesnake's tail. Some animals can even produce sounds that we cannot hear. For example, there are the high-pitched squeaks of bats and mice, and the low-pitched moans of whales in the ocean.

Scientists have found out all they know about sound by doing experiments. When they have an idea about how things work, they think up different experiments to test whether their ideas are right. Scientists then change their ideas to explain the results of their experiments. In this book you will try out some experiments with sound for yourself. Doing experiments is a fun way to learn about science. It will help you find out why the world behaves in the way it does.

The science of sound

Sound is made when something vibrates (moves back and forth very quickly). If you put one of your fingers gently on your throat while you speak, you will feel the vibrations of your vocal cords. These vibrations produce the sound of your voice. The same thing happens when you pluck the string of a guitar. The string moves rapidly from side to side, creating the sound of the musical note.

You can hear someone talking or plucking a guitar string because the sound travels from where it is made and into your ears. Sound is a type of energy that travels between two places by making invisible waves in the air. Sound waves are a bit like the waves that travel across the sea. Imagine someone playing a guitar across the room from you. Now imagine waves of sound, like the waves on the sea, traveling through the air from the guitar to your ears.

LEARNING ABOUT SCIENCE

Doing experiments is the best way to learn about science. This is the way scientists test their ideas and find out new information. Follow this good science guide to get the most out of each experiment in this book.

- Never begin an experiment until you have talked to an adult about what you are going to do.
- Take care when you do or set up an experiment, whether it is dangerous or not. Make sure you know the safety rules before you start work. Wear goggles and use the right safety equipment when you are told to do so.
- Do each experiment more than once. The more times you carry out an experiment, the more accurate your results will be.
- Keep a notebook to record the results of your experiments. Make your results easy to read and understand. You can make notes and draw charts, diagrams, and tables.
- Drawing a graph is a great way of presenting your results. Plot the results of your experiment as dots on a graph. Use a ruler to draw a straight line through all the dots. Reading the graph will help you to fill in the gaps in your experiment.
- Write down the results as you do each experiment. If one result seems different from the rest, you might have made a mistake that you can fix immediately.
- Learn from your mistakes. Some of the most exciting findings in science came from an unexpected result. If your results do not tally with your predictions, try to find out why.

All the sounds of the different musical instruments in an orchestra, from a violin to a trumpet, combine to make the music people like to hear.

Sound waves

Sound waves are a lot like water waves, but they are different in one very important way. Waves carry energy through water because parts of the water move up and down. It is the same as a crowd wave moving around a baseball park. The people do not move left or right, but the wave appears to move around the baseball park as people stand up and sit down. This is the same as water waves in the ocean. The water does not move from left to right—it simply bobs up and down. This type of wave is called a transverse wave.

Sound waves are different. When an object vibrates in the air, the vibrations push on air particles next to the surface of the object. These air particles bounce into neighboring air particles, which bump into more particles and push them along too. This forms a continuous wave, called a compression wave. When sound moves in a compression wave, the individual air particles move back and forth in the same direction as the wave itself.

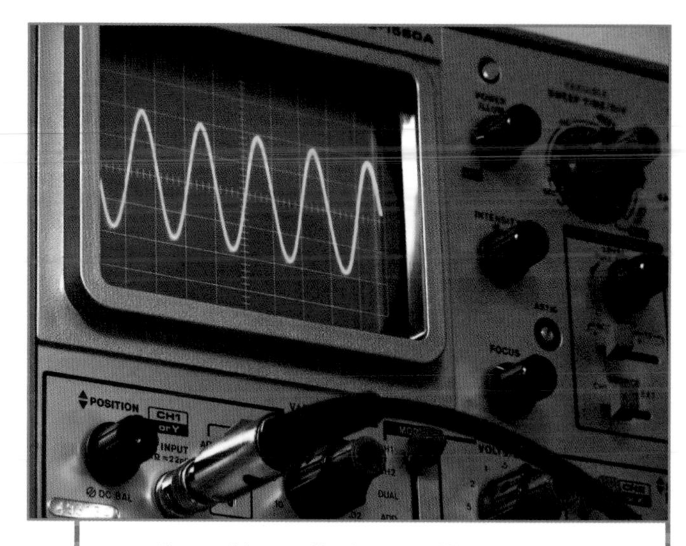

A machine called an oscilloscope draws a picture of what sound waves would look like if we could see them. Louder sounds produce taller waves on the oscilloscope's screen.

Speed of sound

Sound needs something to travel through, such as the air or water. It cannot move in empty space, which is called a vacuum. In a vacuum, there are no molecules to bump into each other and set up a compression wave. The speed of sound in the air at normal temperature is about 770 miles (1,250km) per hour. In water, the sound waves speed up to around 3,130 miles (5,050km) per hour. In a piece of steel, the sound waves travel faster still—at around 11,200 miles (18,000km) per hour. Temperature does not really affect the speed of sound in a solid or liquid, but it does when sound moves through the air. This is because the air particles bump into each other more quickly as the temperature rises, making the sound waves travel much more quickly.

When you talk on the telephone, your voice creates sound vibrations inside the telephone. These vibrations change into electrical signals. The signals change back into sound vibrations at the other end of the line.

BE SAFE!

The experiments in this book are all safe if you follow the instructions very carefully in each one. If you are ever in any doubt about what to do, ask an adult to help you.

Different sounds

There are three things that make sounds different from one another. They are loudness, pitch, and quality. Loudness is a measure of how much energy is in a sound wave. Loud sounds have very large sound waves. Pitch describes whether a sound is high (like a shrill whistle) or low (like a rumble of thunder). The pitch varies as the frequency (number of vibrations every second) of the sound varies. The quality of a sound is what allows people to distinguish the sound of a violin from the sound made by a piano—even if the two musical instruments are playing exactly the same note at the same loudness. The quality of sound depends of the shape of the sound wave.

Hearing sound

The sound waves you can hear when someone beats on a drum or talks to you are collected by your ears and turned into information that your brain can understand. When the sound waves reach your ears, they travel down the ear canal and hit the eardrum. The sound makes the eardrum vibrate. Tiny bones inside the ear pick up the vibrations of the eardrum and make them stronger. The vibrations then pass to a structure called the cochlea deep inside the ear. The cochlea is full of nerves that send messages to the brain.

Having two ears means that your brain can figure out where sounds are coming from and pinpoint the source of a sound very accurately. Some animals, such as rabbits, can lift up their ears and move them around to locate sounds even more accurately. Other animals, like dogs, are sensitive to sounds that people cannot hear.

Measuring sound

Different sounds are all around us, but our brains are very good at picking out the sounds we need to hear and ignoring others. Some sounds are so loud that we cannot ignore them. The loudness of a sound can be measured on a scale of units called decibels. Zero on the decibel scale corresponds to the faintest sound the human ears can hear—like a pin dropping on the ground. The sound of a vacuum cleaner measures about 70 decibels. Pneumatic drills can measure up to 100 decibels. There is no limit on the decibel scale, but our ears cannot listen to sounds greater than about 110 decibels without feeling a lot of pain. Extremely loud sounds, such as an explosion, can actually burst the eardrum inside each ear.

DOPPLER EFFECT

When a fire truck speeds along the street, the sound of the siren changes as the truck moves past you. The sound drops to a lower pitch. This is called the Doppler effect, named for Austrian scientist Christian Johann Doppler (1803–1853). The Doppler effect occurs because the speed of the vehicle affects the speed of the sound waves traveling out from the siren. If you stand in front of the truck, the sound waves will appear to be moving faster and arrive more frequently. The pitch of the siren will be higher. If you stand behind the truck, the sound waves will be appear to be moving slower and arrive less often. The pitch of the siren will be lower.

Bouncing Waves

Goals

1. Make a sound detector.
2. Use it to listen to different sound waves.

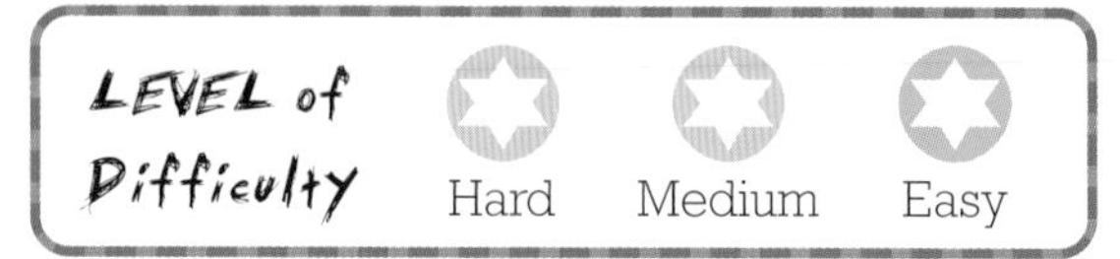

What you will need

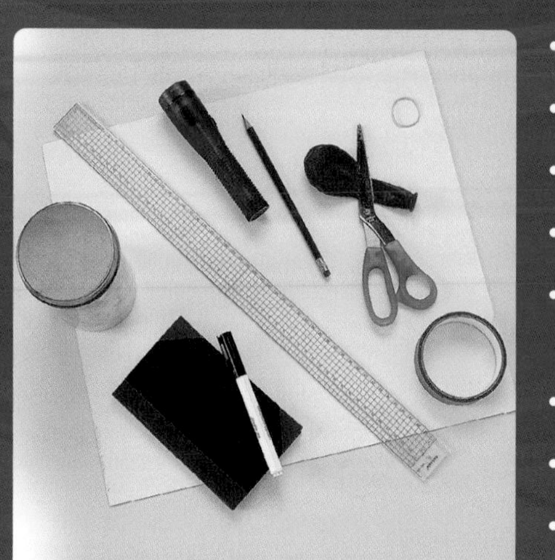

- white card
- pen and pencil
- ruler
- balloon
- large can, open at both ends
- rubber band
- small mirror
- flashlight
- sticky tape

ROBERT BOYLE

Irish chemist Robert Boyle (1627–1691) figured out that sound can only travel through a medium, such as air or water. He set an alarm clock ringing in a large jar. Then he pumped all the air out of the jar. When all the air had been removed, Boyle could no longer hear the clock.

1. Draw a grid of squares on the card. Each square should be 2 × 2 inches (5 × 5cm). Fill the whole sheet with your grid.

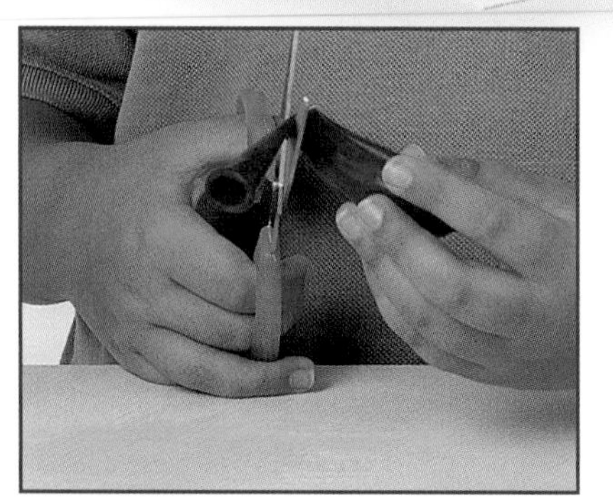

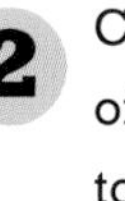

2. Cut the end off the balloon to make a large sheet of rubber.

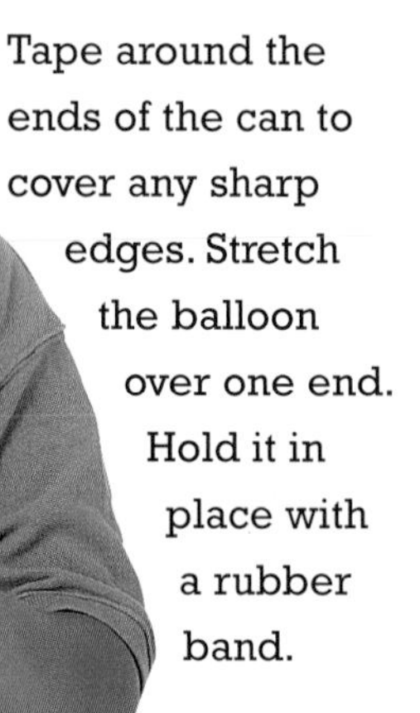

3. Tape around the ends of the can to cover any sharp edges. Stretch the balloon over one end. Hold it in place with a rubber band.

4 Tape the mirror to the balloon.

5 Stand your card grid upright against a pile of books on a table. Put the can and flashlight on the table so that the light from the flashlight shines on the mirror and reflects onto the card.

TROUBLESHOOTING

What if I can't see the light moving?

Darken the room by turning out the lights. Then try moving the flashlight so that it shines more directly onto the mirror. You could also try using dark card, and use tape to make the lines of the grid. Or try making a louder sound.

6 Make a mark in the square where the light is shining.

7 Hold your hands about 2 feet (60cm) away from the can. Clap once while looking at the grid. How far does the light move? Make a mark in the square where the light moves to.

SAFETY TIP!

Take care not to cut yourself when taping around the sharp edges of the can.

8 Clap your hands 6 inches (15cm) away from the can. Make another mark in the square where the light moves to.

9 Measure the distances between the original mark and the two marks you made when you clapped your hands. How far did the light jump?

Spot that Sound

What you will need

- 4 plastic funnels
- scissors
- tape
- ruler or piece of wooden dowel about 3 feet (1m) long
- modeling clay
- stool or chair
- blindfold
- alarm clock, radio, or other source of sound
- a friend
- 2 pieces of flexible plastic tubing, about 4 feet (1.2m) long

Goals

1. Build a simple sound locator.
2. Test how good your locator is at finding sounds.

LEVEL of Difficulty

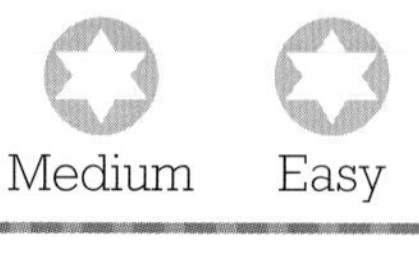

Hard Medium Easy

1 Attach a funnel to each end of the two pieces of plastic tubing.

2 Tape one funnel on each piece of tubing to each end of the ruler.

HEARING AIDS

Before electronic hearing aids were invented, people who were hard of hearing held large "ear trumpets" to their ears. The ear trumpets gathered sounds to make them louder. Try this yourself by cupping your open palms behind your ears. You should be able to hear faint sounds more clearly.

3 Put a piece of modeling clay on the stool. Push the ruler into the clay to hold it in place.

4 Put on the blindfold, and hold the two free funnels to your ears. Ask a friend to hold the sound source (here, an alarm clock). He or she can also record the results in a notebook.

TROUBLESHOOTING

What if I can't locate the sound properly?

Check that the plastic tubing hasn't twisted around on itself, because this could block the sound waves from reaching your ears. Your friend might be standing too far away from the funnels. Ask him or her to move a little bit closer.

SURROUND SOUND

Action movies use "surround sound" to make it seem more realistic. Loudspeakers positioned around the movie theater can make sounds appear to come from anywhere—even behind the audience.

SAFETY TIP!

Don't hold the alarm too close to the funnels as the sound could damage your ears.

5 Your friend should stand somewhere in the room and set off the alarm clock. Keep the blindfold on. Point toward the sound when you think you know where it is coming from.

6 Repeat this activity a few more times. Ask your friend to keep a note of where he or she was standing, and if you correctly located the sound.

Measuring Sound

Goals

1. Measure the speed of sound.
2. Calculate the speed of sound yourself.

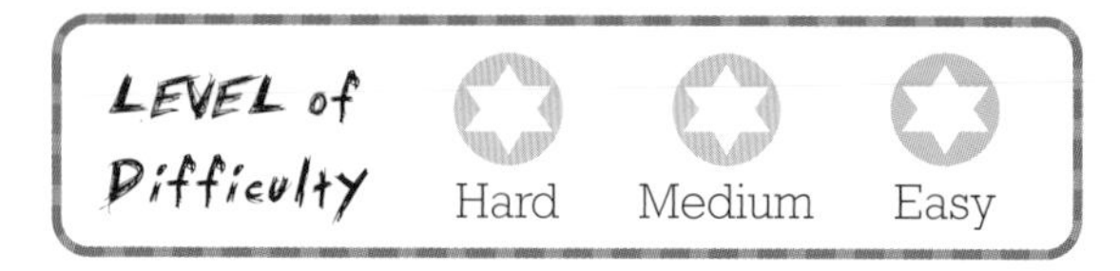

What you will need

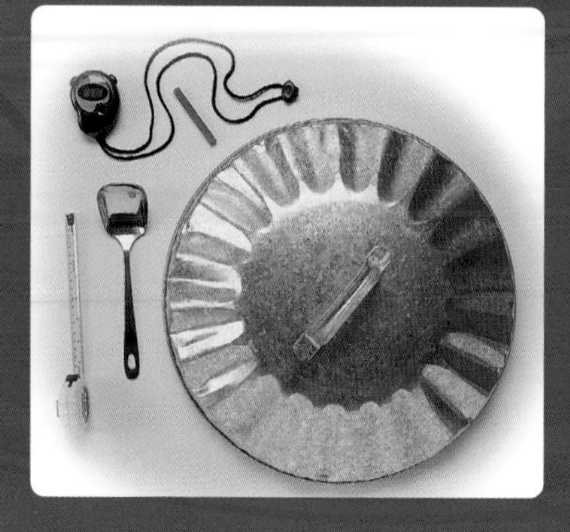

- measuring tape
- a wall outside with a large empty space around it
- chalk
- lid of a trashcan
- spoon
- stopwatch

ACCURATE EXPERIMENTS

In this activity you will measure the time it takes sound to travel to the wall and back 20 times. You could just measure the time between one sound and one echo. Measuring the sound 20 times makes the experiment much more accurate. It gives you more time to stop the clock accurately.

1. Mark the ground with chalk 150 feet (45.7m) away from the wall. Measure the distance as accurately as you can. Repeat this measurement from the same place as before. Mark the distance on the floor again. If the two marks are not in exactly the same place, draw a line halfway between them. This will make your distance measurement more accurate.

2 Stand on the chalk mark next to your friend, facing the wall. One person starts the stopwatch at the same time as the other person makes a sharp noise by banging on the lid of the trashcan.

3 As soon as you hear the echo, make another noise with the lid of the trashcan. Repeat this 20 times. After you have banged the trashcan lid 20 times, listen for the last echo. When you hear it, stop the watch. Write down the the total time taken for the experiment in minutes and seconds. Divide the total distance traveled by the sound by the time on the stopwatch to work out the speed of sound.

TROUBLESHOOTING

Why is my measurement way off what it should be?

Your speed of sound measurement should be around 1,000 feet (300m) per second. If your results are way off, repeat the experiment a few times and take an average reading. This will make the final result more accurate.

The first person to measure the speed of sound in air was French mathematician Marin Mersenne (1588–1648). In 1640, he figured out that sound travels at 1,000 feet (300m) per second, which is close to the value of 1,128 feet (344m) per second. Scientists accept this as the speed of sound today.

Tuning Fork

What you will need

- bucket about two-thirds full of water
- long plastic or card tube open at both ends
- tuning forks of several different pitches
- ruler and pen

Goals

1. Measure the wavelength of sounds made inside a tube.
2. See how the wavelength of the sound depends on the pitch of the tuning fork.

LEVEL of Difficulty: Hard Medium Easy

1 Put the tube into the bucket of water so it is upright and almost submerged. Strike one of the tuning forks on a table top. Hold the tuning fork over the end of the tube poking out of the water.

2 Keep the fork held just above the tube opening. Listen as you pull the tube out of the water. Keep listening until you find a point where the sound is loudest.

3 Mark the side of the tube when you find the point where the sound is loudest.

STANDING WAVE

When a standing wave forms inside a tube, the wavelength is one-quarter the size of a full wave.

4 Take the tube out of the water. Measure the distance from the mark to the top of the tube (the end that has not been in the water). Write down the result in your notebook.

TROUBLESHOOTING

What if you don't hear any changes in the sound?

The change in volume may not be as loud as you might expect. Repeat the experiment in a quiet room, and listen very closely. If it still doesn't work, your tube may not be long enough. Try again with a longer tube.

When people walk over a bridge or the wind blows against it, the bridge vibrates. If the vibration is at or near the bridge's resonant frequency, the bridge can vibrate so violently that it tears itself apart. Resonance caused the collapse of the suspension bridge over the Tacoma Narrows in Washington State in 1940.

5 Put the tube back in the water. Keep moving it up and down until you find a second spot where the sound is loudest. Mark it with a pen.

6 Measure the distance from the second mark to the end of the tube. Record this distance. Now take a tuning fork of a different pitch. Repeat steps 1 to 4. Each time, write down your results in your notebook.

Sound Through a Balloon

Goals

1. Slow down sound waves.
2. See how sound waves move through different gases.

What you will need

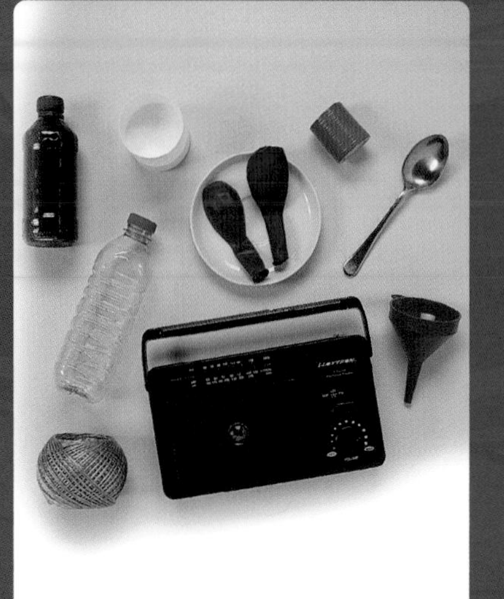

- plastic bottle with a narrow neck
- funnel
- tablespoon
- baking powder
- vinegar
- balloon
- string
- sticky tape
- saucer
- radio

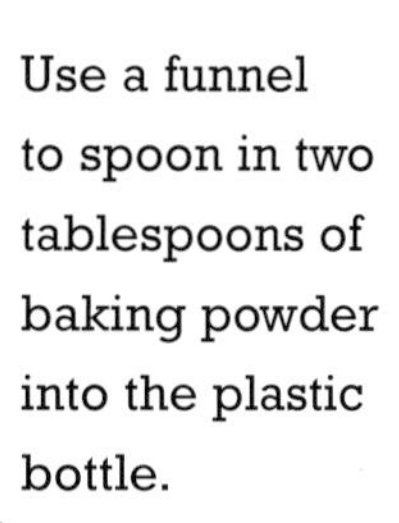

1 Use a funnel to spoon in two tablespoons of baking powder into the plastic bottle.

2 Add some vinegar. A chemical reaction takes place, and carbon dioxide gas is produced.

SAFETY TIP!
Take care when mixing the baking powder and the vinegar!

3 Stretch a balloon over the neck of the bottle as soon as the reaction starts. The balloon will inflate with the carbon dioxide gas.

4 Tie the neck securely when the balloon is fully inflated.

TROUBLESHOOTING

I found it hard to tell whether the sound was louder with the balloon in place or removed.

Cover up your other ear (the one farthest away from the radio) or block it completely with a foam earplug. Sound reaching this ear might not be traveling through the balloon—it might be bouncing off the walls). This could interfere with your results.

5 Tape the balloon onto the saucer so that it does not move.

6 Put the radio on a table about 1.5 feet (45cm) from the balloon. Switch the radio on and turn it up quite loud. Put your ear to the other side of the balloon. Move your head until you find the point where the sound is loudest. Turn down the radio until you can barely hear it. If you cannot reach, ask a friend to turn it down while you listen.

The effects of helium on sound can be heard by divers. They breathe a mixture of oxygen and helium instead of normal air, which is mostly a mixture of oxygen and nitrogen. It keeps them from getting the painful condition called the bends when they come to the surface. But the helium makes the divers speak with funny squeaky voices.

7 Take away the balloon. Does the radio sound louder or quieter?

Make a String Instrument

What you will need

- large, empty can
- hook
- modeling clay
- ruler
- elastic
- plastic bottle
- set of weights, such as some identical metal nuts or identical coins

Goals

1. Make a string instrument.
2. Investigate how the pitch of the notes changes as you change the length and tightness of the string.

1 Push or screw the hook into the can, about 1–2 inches (2.5–5cm) to one side.

2 Use modeling clay to stick the ruler to the opposite edge of the can. The ruler should stand on one of its long edges.

SAFETY TIP!

If you use an elastic band for your string, make sure you use eye protection or stand well back when you pluck it in case the band breaks.

3 Cut a length of elastic. Tie one end around the hook. Tie the other end to the plastic bottle. Drop a few weights into the bottle. Hang it over the ruler. Put the can at the edge of a table to make this easier.

TROUBLESHOOTING

What if I can't get a good sound from the elastic?

You may find that thick elastic does not produce a clear twanging sound, like a guitar string. You can use a rubber band instead. You can also try using thick string or twine.

5 Put more weights in the bottle. What difference does this make to the sound of the note. Repeat the experiment several times with different weights. Add the same extra weight each time. What do you notice about the way the note changes?

4 Pluck the elastic with your finger. Listen to the note that it makes.

Straw Pipes

Goals

1. Produce a standing wave in a pipe that is open at both ends.
2. See how the wavelength and pitch of the sound depends on the length of the pipe.

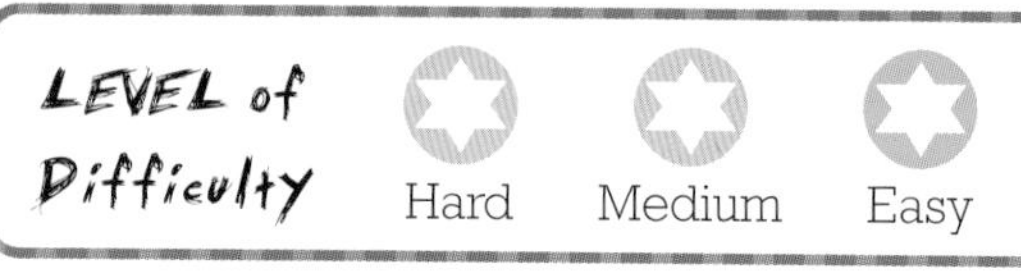

What you will need

- drinking straws
- ruler
- pen
- scissors
- sticky tape

1 Take a straw. Use the ruler to measure 1 inch (2.5cm) from one end. Draw a line on the straw to mark this point.

2 Cut the straw where you made the line. Throw the smaller piece away.

3 Repeat steps one and two with six more straws. Make each straw one inch shorter than the last.

4 Line the straws up in order of length, from longest to shortest. Tape them all together to make your straw pipe.

SAFETY TIP!

Take care when using scissors. Always cut away from your body.

TROUBLESHOOTING

What if I can't make any sound?

It takes a little practice to blow across the top of the pipes properly, so keep experimenting. If your pipe still doesn't work, you may be using straws that are too thin or too short. Try making another set of pipes using different straws.

STANDING WAVE

In this activity you are making a simple set of pipes out of drinking straws. There's nothing to keep you from adding as many pipes as you want, but you have a long way to go to match the world's biggest pipe instrument. That record belongs to the pipe organ at the Atlantic City Convention Hall in New Jersey. It contains about 32,000 separate pipes. The largest one is 64 feet (19.5m) long and 3 feet (1m) around at the top. It was carved from a single tree!

5 Blow across the top of your pipe. Notice how the pitch changes as the straws get shorter or longer.

Toot Together

What you will need

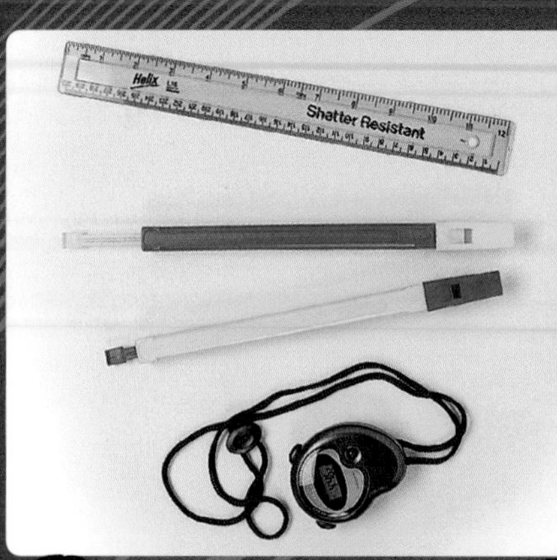

- 2 slide whistles (whistles with movable pistons that change the sounds they make)
- 12-inch (30-cm) ruler
- stopwatch
- a friend

Goals

1. Add together two different sounds to produce beats.
2. See how the beat changes over time.

LEVEL of Difficulty

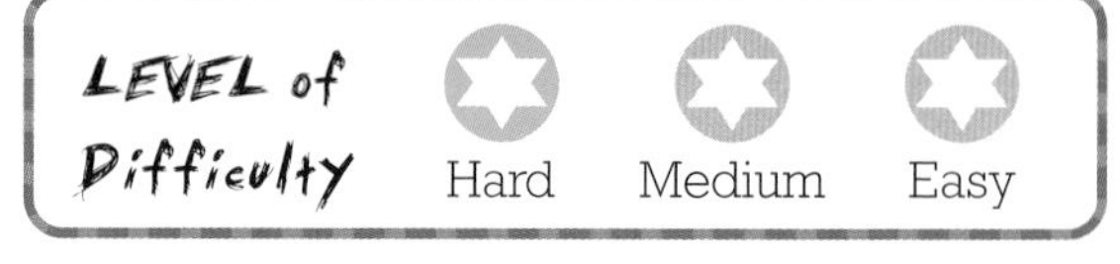

SAFETY TIP!

Do not push a whistle into someone's mouth while they are blowing it.

1. Take one whistle, and give the other one to your friend. Pull the piston of each whistle out halfway. Ask your friend to blow into his or her whistle and play the same note. Move the piston of your whistle until your note matches the note your friend is playing.

2. Pull the piston of your whistle out slowly. You should be able to hear the volume of the sounds produced by the two whistles rising and falling in beats. Pull your piston even farther out so the two notes differ even more. You will notice the changes in volume happen more quickly until you can no longer hear them. What happens as you push the piston back in again?

3. Repeat step one, but this time measure the length of pistons sticking out from your whistles.

4. Slowly pull the piston out of your whistle until you begin to hear beats. Start the stopwatch when the beats are loudest. Measure the time it takes to make ten beats.

5. Write down the time it takes to make ten beats together with the distance that the piston is sticking out of your whistle.

TROUBLESHOOTING

What if I can't hear any beats or if they aren't regular?

To make the beats regular, the two notes must join together to make them regular, too. Make sure that you and your friend blow into your whistles with a steady, even breath so the notes that you make have a constant volume.

TUNING PIANOS

Piano tuners use beats to tune pianos. Each string in the piano is compared with strings that produce notes of similar pitch. By listening for beats when two strings play at once, a skilled piano tuner can tell exactly how much each string needs adjusting.

6. Pull your piston out a little farther until you notice the beats have speeded up a little. Write down the time it takes to make ten beats. Don't forget to measure how far your piston is sticking out of the whistle.

7. Keep repeating step 6 until you can no longer hear any beats.

Muffling Sound

Goals

1. Compare how well different materials insulate sound.
2. Learn how to reduce sound.

What you will need

- small radio
- different materials, such as card, padded envelopes, rubber sheeting, and polystyrene
- sticky tape
- cushion or pillow
- ruler
- scissors

SOUNDPROOFING BUILDINGS

Soundproofing insulates buildings from unwanted sounds. The outer walls are very heavy, because they do not let sound through as easily as lighter walls. The windows are made of several layers of glass with spaces between. Air conditioning allows the windows to be kept closed. Insulation in the walls and double floors also help to soundproof buildings.

1 Cut out pieces of different material so that they are slightly bigger than the speaker of the radio—about a half-inch (1.5cm) all the way around.

2 Cover the speaker in the same way for each material. The thickness of each material should be at least a half-inch (1.5cm). For thinner materials, cut several pieces. Put them one on top of another until you have the same thickness.

TROUBLESHOOTING

I can't find a big difference between the materials.

This experiment will give you a rough idea about the type of materials that block sound. However, it may not be very precise. It might be hard to judge the loudness of the sounds from the radio and to read the volume scale accurately. Try making the thickness of each material greater and repeat the experiment several times to see if you get the same results.

3 Put one of the materials over the speaker. Rest the radio on a cushion to absorb sounds coming from the back. Turn down the radio until you can't hear the sound. Read the number on the volume knob, and write it in a table next to the name of the material.

4 Repeat step 3 with each material.

KILLING SOUND

One amazing type of ear guard actually kills off unwanted sounds. Electronic circuits measure the unwanted sound and then generate "antisound" inside the earphones. The antisound is identical to the unwanted sound, but the waves are out of step with the original waves. The waves of sound and antisound cancel each other out, and the wearer of the earphones hears no sound at all.

Build a Bullroarer

What you will need

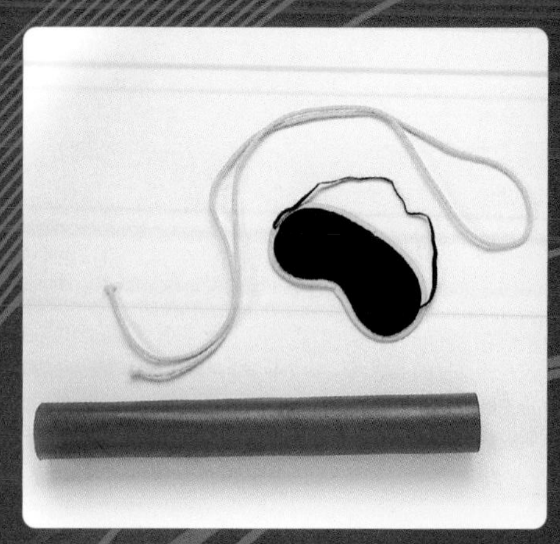

- card tube or strip of thick card made into a tube
- 3-foot (1-m) length of thick string
- blindfold
- a friend

Goals

1 Make a sound generator called a bullroarer.

2 Use your bullroarer to test the Doppler effect.

LEVEL of Difficulty: Hard Medium Easy

SAFETY TIP!

The forces acting on the bullroarer increase the faster you swing it around. Make sure you tie the string securely to the card tube. It's best to do this experiment outside so you don't damage or break anything. Make sure that you and your friend stand a safe distance apart. Remember that one of you is wearing a blindfold and could stray into the path of the bullroarer!

1 Ask an adult to make two holes at one end of the tube. Thread the string through the holes. Tie it securely.

2 You will operate the bullroarer. Your friend will listen to the sound it makes.

3 You and your friend should stand about 30 feet (10m) apart. Swing the bullroarer around your head at a steady speed. Make a sound that has a continuous pitch. It is important that the sound you make has the same pitch throughout the experiment.

4 Ask your friend to wear a blindfold and listen to the pitch of the note.

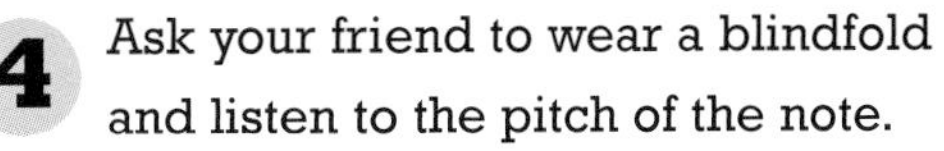

5 Walk along a straight line in front of your friend, while you swing the bullroarer at a constant speed. Your friend should try to spot the moment when you walk past him or her by listening for a shift in the pitch of the bullroarer. This is called the Doppler effect.

6 Swap roles with your friend, and repeat the experiment.

TROUBLESHOOTING

What if my friend can't hear the Doppler effect?

Swing the bullroarer at a constant speed throughout the activity. If you change the speed, the pitch of the sound the bullroarer makes will vary. Then you will be unable to pinpoint the Doppler effect. You can also try swinging the bullroarer more quickly. Then you should hear the Doppler effect more clearly. You could also try using a different device to generate sound. It should make continuous loud notes at the same frequency. A pitch pipe would work well. Or you could use an instrument such as a recorder and play one long note.

Making Thunder

Goals

1. Make your own bolt of lightning.
2. Hear your own tiny rumble of thunder.

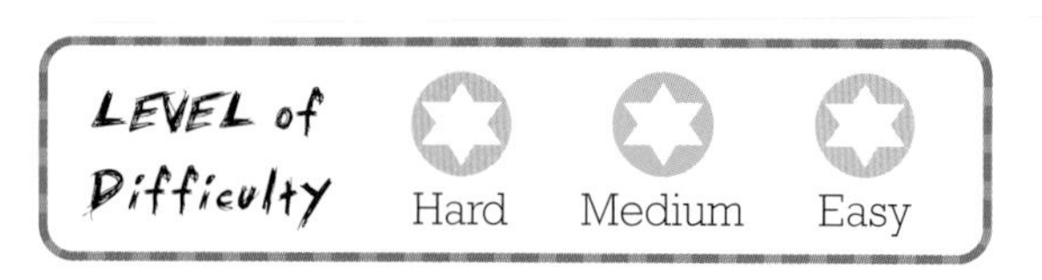

What you will need

- plastic sheet
- sticky tape
- rubber gloves
- large iron or steel cooking pot (not aluminum) with a plastic handle
- iron or steel fork
- plastic ruler

1. Tape the plastic sheet onto a tabletop.

2. Put on the rubber gloves.

BENJAMIN FRANKLIN

In the eighteenth century, U.S. scientist Benjamin Franklin (1706–1790) did some experiments with electricity. In one experiment, he flew a silk kite in a thunderstorm. His kite carried a metal rod, which was attached to a long piece of twine tied to a key. During the storm Franklin was able to charge a Leyden jar with electricity from the kite. Many scientists tried to repeat Franklin's experiment and were electrocuted. Franklin was very lucky not to have been killed. NEVER fly a kite during a thunderstorm.

3 Hold the cooking pot by its handle. Rub it on the plastic sheet.

TROUBLESHOOTING

What if I can't see the spark?

The spark of static electricity that you make is very small. You will be able to see it better if you carry out the experiment in a dark room.

4 Take the fork in your other hand. Bring the fork near to the cooking pot. A tiny spark of static electricity should jump across the gap between the pot and the fork. You should be able to hear the spark as it jumps. This is like a tiny rumble of thunder.

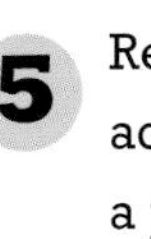

5 Repeat the activity using a plastic ruler instead of a fork. What happens now?

SAFETY TIP!

Try to use a pot with an insulating handle and wear rubber gloves because the pan will keep the charge.

Glossary

aluminum: a type of metal

bends: also called decompression sickness. The bends occurs when a diver rises to the surface of the water too quickly and bubbles of gas form in his or her blood.

carbon dioxide: a colorless, odorless gas

cochlea: a tube inside the ear in which sound vibrations change into nerve signals

compression wave: also called a longitudinal wave. A compression wave vibrates in the same direction in which it moves.

decibel: the unit of measurement for the loudness of sound

Doppler effect: the apparent change in the frequency of a sound wave as the source of the sound moves toward or away from someone listening to it

echo: the reflection of a sound wave

frequency: the number of times a sound vibrates in a given time

gas: one of the states of matter. Gases have no fixed volume and no shape.

insulation: in sound, a material that helps to reduce unwanted sounds

iron: a type of metal

jet engine: an engine that burns fuel to create a stream of hot gas to push an object, such as a jet plane, forward

liquid: one of the states of matter. Liquids have a fixed volume but no shape, so they take the shape of their container.

oscilloscope: a machine that can be used to "see" sound waves by converting them into electrical signals

pitch: the property of sound that varies as the frequency of sound vibration varies

resonance: when a very large vibration is caused by a smaller vibration because the frequencies are the same

solid: one of the states of matter. Solids have both a fixed volume and shape.

speed: the distance traveled in a given time

standing wave: also called a stationary wave. A standing wave occurs when two waves combine with each other to produce a wave that appears to stay in the same place.

static electricity: an electric charge that does not move from one place to another

steel: a very strong type of iron

supersonic: faster than the speed of sound

temperature: a measure of the heat in something

transverse wave: a wave that moves up and down as it travels through a medium, such as air or water

vacuum: a completely empty space

vibration: movement from side to side about a fixed point

wavelength: the distance between one peak of a wave to the peak of the next wave

Further Information

Books

Cook, Trevor. *Experiments with Light and Sound.* New York: PowerKids Press, 2009.

Oxlade, Chris. *Experiments with Sound: Explaining Sound.* Mankato, MN: Heinemann-Raintree, 2009.

Parker, Steve. *The Science of Sound: Projects and Experiments with Music and Sound Waves.* Mankato, MN: Heineman-Raintree, 2005.

Spilsbury, Richard, and Louise Spilsbury. *What Is Sound?: Exploring Science With Hands-on Activities.* Berkeley Heights, NJ: Enslow Elementary, 2008.

Tocci, Salvatore. *Experiments with Sound.* New York: Children's Press, 2002.

Websites

www.smm.org/sound/nocss/activity/top.html

www.exploratorium.edu/music/

www.bbc.co.uk/schools/scienceclips/ages/9_10/changing_sounds.shtml

Index